NICK BUTTERWORTH AND MICK INKPEN

STORIES JESUS TOLD

To help people understand what God is like,
Jesus told lots of stories which are as exciting
today as when they were first heard.

The Lost Sheep is still a great favourite
and its message is one that children especially
love to hear.

Marshall Pickering
An Imprint of HarperCollins*Publishers*
77–85 Fulham Palace Road,
Hammersmith, London W6 8JB, UK
1   3   5   7   9   10   8   6   4   2

First published by Marshall Morgan & Scott in 1986
This edition published in 1994 by Marshall Pickering

A catalogue record for this book is available
from The British Library

0-551-02873-4

Printed in Singapore

Co-edition arranged by Angus Hudson Ltd, London

The Lost Sheep

Nick Butterworth and Mick Inkpen

Marshall Pickering
An Imprint of HarperCollinsPublishers

Here is a farmer.
He has a hundred sheep.
He is counting them.

One of his sheep is missing.
Oh dear!
Where has it gone?

Is it in the hen-house?
No.

Is it behind the haystack?
No.

Is it under the hedge?
No, it is lost.

All day the farmer looks
for his sheep.
He climbs up hills and
scrambles over rocks.

He crawls through bramble
bushes.
The thorns scratch him.
But he will not give up.

He is tired and hungry.
His feet ache.
But he will not give up.

At last, the farmer sees
his sheep.
It has fallen in the river.

The farmer dives into
the water.
Splosh!
He rescues the sheep.

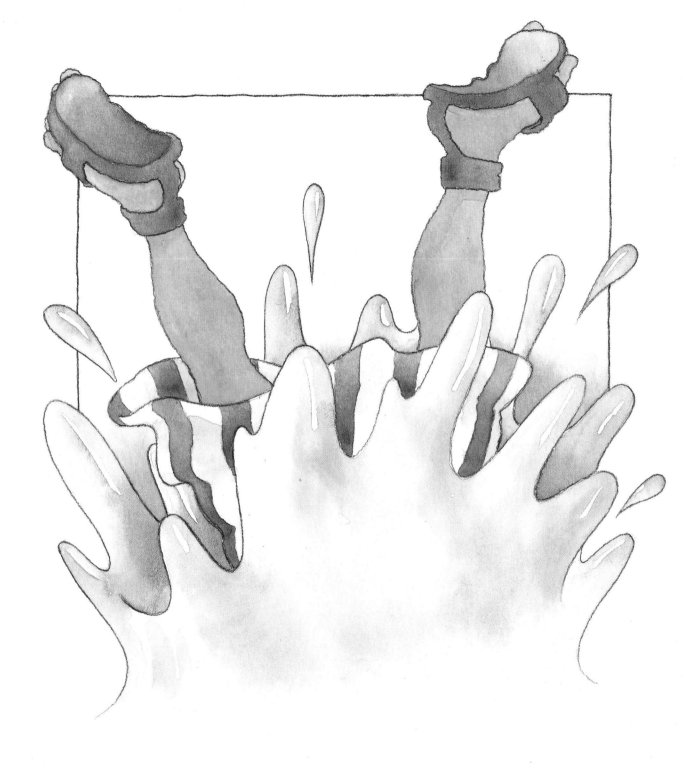

Hooray! The farmer has found
his sheep.
Let's all have a party!

Jesus says, 'God is like
the farmer. He loves us
just like the farmer loves
his sheep.'

You can read the story of **The Lost Sheep** in Luke chapter 15 verses 1 to 7.